HOW I
CHANGED
*the* WORLD

# Mohandas Gandhi

WORLD
BOOK

World Book, Inc.
180 North LaSalle Street
Suite 900
Chicago, Illinois 60601
USA

For information about other "How I Changed the World" titles, as well as other World Book print and digital publications, please go to **www.worldbook.com**.

For information about other World Book publications, call 1-800-WORLDBK (967-5325).

For information about sales to schools and libraries, call 1-800-975-3250 (United States) or 1-800-837-5365 (Canada).

Library of Congress Cataloging-in-Publication Data for this volume has been applied for.

How I Changed the World
ISBN: 978-0-7166-2278-9 (set, hc.)

Mohandas Gandhi
ISBN: 978-0-7166-2281-9 (hc.)

Also available as:
ISBN: 978-0-7166-2287-1 (e-book)

Printed in China by Shenzhen Wing King Tong Paper Products Co., Ltd., Shenzhen, Guangdong
1st printing July 2018

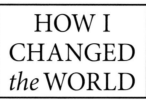

HOW I
CHANGED
*the* WORLD

# Mohandas Gandhi

WORLD
BOOK

# CONTENTS

# CHAPTER 1

# Student of Law

## Early Childhood in India

Mohandas Karamchand Gandhi was an Indian lawyer, social activist, and writer who led the movement that won his country's independence from the British Empire. Commonly referred to as the *Mahatma* (meaning Great Soul in the ancient Indian Sanskrit language), he is widely loved and respected in India today as the Father of the Nation. Gandhi helped to gain India's *sovereignty*, or independence, through nonviolent means and civil disobedience. (Civil disobedience is the deliberate and public refusal to obey a law because of one's principles.) Gandhi continues to inspire civil rights movements throughout the world.

Mohandas was born on Oct. 2, 1869, in Porbandar, a small town in western India on the coast of the Arabian Sea. His father, Karamchand (also known as Kaba), served as the *diwan* (chief minister) of India's princely state of Porbandar (today the state of Gujarat). (Local Indian princes ruled princely states, or native states of India.) Kaba, who had an elementary education, had previously served as a governmental clerk. His first two wives both died at a young age and had each given him a daughter. In 1857, Kaba sought permission from his third wife to remarry. That same year, he married his fourth wife, Putlibai. She was only 15 at the time, more than 25 years Kaba's junior, and a deeply religious woman. Over the next 10 years, the couple had four children, three boys and a girl. Their elder son, Lakshmidas, was born in 1860. He later earned a law degree and entered Porbandar's financial services. Their daughter, Raliatbehn, was born in 1862 and helped to care for the young Mohandas after

Mohandas's father, Karamchand Gandhi (left), served as the *diwan* (chief minister) of the princely states of Porbandar and Rajkot in western India.

he was born. Kaba and Putlibai's second son, Karsandas, was born in 1866. He joined the police force of the neighboring state of Rajkot later in life.

Mohandas was Kaba and Putlibai's last child. The Gandhi family were faithful Hindus and therefore strict vegetarians. They also belonged to the Bania (merchant) community of India's *caste* system, a rigid social structure determined by a person's birth. (The name *Gandhi* means "perfume seller.") The merchant caste was generally known for its wealth, thrift, business skills, and honesty. Mohandas was spoiled from the day of his birth by his mother, sister, half-sisters, and the family's *aiya* (nanny). He grew up thinking that women's role in society was to be subservient, which means to do as they were told. Naturally, he was also greatly influenced by his mother's beliefs. Putlibai always prayed before meals and was particularly strict about her diet, observing daily religious fasts. Years later, Mohandas found inspiration in his mother's fasting and used it as a political weapon.

In 1874, Kaba moved from the coastal town of Porbandar to the princely state of Rajkot, more than 100 miles away, leaving his family behind. There, he served as an adviser to Rajkot's ruler, Thakur Sahib.

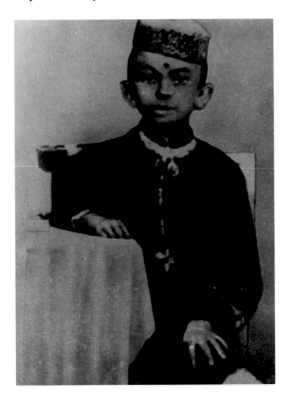

Mohandas was an average but shy student in school, with little interest in sports. Below is a photograph of Mohandas as a young boy around 7 years old.

Kaba's new position in Rajkot was considered less prestigious than the one he had held in Porbandar, but this move came with many opportunities. For one thing, the regional British government was stationed in Rajkot, and Kaba's new assignment gave him and his family greater security. Two years later, Kaba became the chief minister of Rajkot, and his family soon joined him there.

At the age of 11, Mohandas was enrolled in Alfred High School in Rajkot. He studied arithmetic, geography, history, and Gujarati, his native language. Mohandas also began to learn English and played cricket. He was an average student. However, he succeeded in winning a few awards. With a shy manner, he had little interest in games and instead chose to focus on his studies.

## Arranged Marriage and Family Life

Following Indian custom, Kaba began looking for a bride on Mohandas's behalf. Arranged marriage was a tradition followed by most of the families in India at the time, and that tradition continues today. By now, Kaba had two unmarried children left, Karsandas and Mohandas. Because Kaba's brother, Tulsidas, also had an unmarried son, the two men pooled their resources. In May 1883, all three weddings took place at the same time in Porbandar. Mohandas and his bride, Kasturbai Makhanji Kapadia, were just 13 and 14 years old, respectively. Mohandas came to refer to Kasturbai affectionately as "Ba." She had been chosen five years earlier by the parents of the two children, in consultation with Hindu priests and astrologers. As Kaba was racing from Rajkot to Porbandar to attend the wedding, he was nearly killed in a terrible accident. The coach he was riding in overturned and threw him to the ground. He suffered several broken bones. At the wedding, his face was covered in bandages, and he was forced to remain seated during the entire ceremony.

Due to his upbringing and his views toward women, Mohandas naturally assumed that his new wife would do whatever he desired without any argument. Kasturbai, however, proved to be more than a match for her new husband. Though she never received a formal education, Kasturbai was just as determined as he was. She was also wiser, in many ways more compassionate, and braver. (Mohandas was still afraid to sleep in the dark.) As was the tradition at the time, Kasturbai spent much of her time at her parents' house. This forced separation turned Mohandas into a jealous, possessive husband. While he could go anywhere he wanted, he would not allow Kasturbai to go anywhere without his permission.

Kasturbai also tried to warn her husband when she saw him heading into danger. Usually, her warnings went unheeded, however. While in high school, Mohandas began to associate with Sheikh Mehtab, the best friend of his brother Karsandas. Mehtab, an older Muslim boy, was the son of the chief of police in Rajkot and became Mohandas's first hero. Mehtab was much bigger than Mohandas and encouraged him to violate his Hindu dietary restrictions and eat meat so that he could grow taller. One day, Mehtab took Mohandas to a *brothel* (a house of prostitution; a place where men pay women for sexual activity), which caused the younger boy long-lasting mental agony. Eventually, Kasturbai convinced her husband that Mehtab was a bad influence.

In 1885, Mohandas's father suffered a serious illness. His condition worsened day by day. Though he received treatment from various doctors, his condition never improved. Mohandas, his mother, and his siblings did everything they could to ease his pain. Kaba died at the age of 63. He passed away in the middle of the night, shortly after Mohandas had come by to check on him. Mohandas was deeply saddened that he had not been there for his father in his final moments. Adding to the tremendous grief he experienced over his father's death, Mohandas's first child, to whom Kasturbai had given birth only a few days earlier, also died suddenly. These two losses left Mohandas in anguish. It would be three years before he and Kasturbai would have another child. Their son Harilal was born in 1888. Three more boys would follow: Manilal, born in 1892; Ramdas, born in 1897; and Devdas, born in 1900.

In November 1887, Mohandas graduated from high school. He had to travel to Ahmedabad, the capital of the state of Gujarat and a city of over 100,000 people, to take his final exam. The 18-year-old Mohandas had spent his whole life between the much smaller cities of Porbandar and Rajkot. To him, Ahmedabad was the busiest, most exciting place he had ever visited, with its marble palaces, British bungalows, and lush gardens. Ahmedabad's inhabitants intrigued him as well. He saw *Parsees* wearing turbans, Jews with long beards, Christian missionaries in their stiff collars, and wealthy Hindu

Mohandas was just 13 and Kasturbai was 14 when they wed in an arranged marriage in 1883. He and his wife are pictured here in South Africa in 1913.

merchants. (Parsees, also spelled Parsis, are members of a religious community in India who are descended from Persian immigrants.) Mohandas was so enchanted by Ahmedabad that he later established his first *ashram*, a place for spiritual retreat in Hinduism, in one of the city's suburbs.

After high school, Mohandas's first plan was to succeed his father as chief adviser to one of Gujarat's princes. He also briefly considered studying medicine, after having nursed his father on his deathbed. Though caring for his father had been a traumatic experience for Mohandas, it sparked in him a desire to serve the sick and disabled. This desire remained with him for the rest of his life. However, his brother Lakshmidas encouraged him to follow in his footsteps and pursue a law degree. Mavji Dave Joshi, a shrewd Brahmin (a member of the priestly caste) and friend to the Gandhi family, also advised Mohandas to become a barrister (lawyer). That meant Mohandas would have to study in London.

> *... his brother Lakshmidas encouraged him to follow in his footsteps and pursue a law degree.*

Mohandas was excited at the prospect of living in London. It was the fabled capital of the British Empire, the home of Queen Victoria, and a city of over five million people at the time. Mohandas began his long journey by making his way to Bombay (known today as Mumbai). Bombay was India's commercial center and gateway to the West. Once a month, a giant steamship entered Bombay's harbor, taking its passengers to and from the British Isles. The elders of Mohandas's Hindu merchant caste were shocked that one of their own wished to travel across the "black waters" of the ocean to London, whose "sinful" inhabitants ate beef and drank wine. They even threatened to banish him from their community if he went, but Mohandas was not discouraged by their threats or stern warnings. Putlibai was also worried for her son, but she was more concerned about the dangers posed to his health than to his soul. On Putlibai's behalf, Mohandas's uncle, Tulsidas, tried to persuade him not to study abroad. To reassure his mother, Mohandas promised not to touch "wine, women or meat" while in the British capital. In the end, Putlibai gave Mohandas her permission to go. By the time he left for England, Mohandas's family included a new addition. His son Harilal was born a few months before his departure. The farewell was a tearful one.

## British Barrister

In late September 1888, Mohandas arrived in Southampton, England, aboard the SS *Clyde*, three days before his 19th birthday. His world was about to expand in ways that he could not have imagined. After going ashore, he made his way to London, where he contacted one of his late father's friends, Dr. P. J. Mehta, who helped familiarize young Mohandas with his new environment. At the time, London was the world's largest city, more than twice the size of Paris, France, or New York City, New York. Its inhabitants included people from almost every nation on Earth. There was also a small Indian community in the city, most of whom studied either business or law. Howev-

Mohandas (right) was encouraged by his brother Lakshmidas (left) to pursue a law degree. Lakshmidas also spent a small fortune on Mohandas's education.

er, Mohandas did not confine himself to London's Indian community. Before starting his legal studies, Mohandas dedicated himself to learning the local customs and was transformed into a proper English gentleman, at least in appearance. He began wearing a "chimney-pot" hat (top hat) and a black bow tie. He also paid for private lessons in public speaking and learned how to dance, play the violin, and speak French. All of this helped him to overcome his childhood shyness as well. Beneath the surface, however,

Mohandas remained a devout Hindu and began reading the *Bhagavad Gita* (meaning "Song of the Blessed One" in Sanskrit), a 700-verse heroic poem that forms part of Hindu scripture.

Two months after arriving in England, Mohandas began his legal studies at London's famed Inner Temple. It was the largest and most costly of London's four ancient Inns of Court. (The *Inns of Court* was the name given during the Middle Ages to four groups of buildings where lawyers lived, studied, taught, and held court.) There were four terms per year, and every aspiring barrister was required to spend at least three years studying law and be 21 years of age when they were "called to the bar." Ironically, Mohandas's education in law provided the foundation for his career as a leader in the Indian independence movement. His studies taught him all about the concepts of liberty and justice and their far-reaching significance. Years later, as he rallied his millions of followers to demand freedom from British control, Mohandas called upon the many lessons he had learned while studying law in London.

*His studies taught him all about the concepts of liberty and justice and their far-reaching significance.*

In June 1891, Mohandas took his final exams and was called to the bar. (The phrase *called to the bar* had its origin in the Inns of Court. Students became full-fledged barristers when they were finally allowed to leave their seat in the outer court and present a legal case at the wooden rail, or *bar*.) Shortly afterward, Mohandas left London for India. On July 5, he reached Bombay, where he was greeted by Lakshmidas. Mohandas's happy reunion with his older brother was tempered by the sad news that Lakshmidas gave him upon his arrival. Their mother had recently died. Mohandas accepted her passing calmly and did not shed a tear. Making his way to the city of Nasik, he performed a Hindu purification there and then returned to his family in Rajkot. As soon as he was reunited with Kasturbai, Mohandas's feelings of jealousy returned in full force. He was suspicious of every excursion his wife made. At the age of 22, he was a self-important, passionate young man with a high opinion of himself and not yet the Mahatma he would one day become.

*When Mohandas appeared in his first court case, his "heart sank into [his] boots."*

The young barrister was now determined to "reform" his uneducated wife and son, as well as his nieces and nephews. He attempted to teach them English. He also insisted that his family dress according to English fashion and introduced Western utensils at the dinner table. All of this proved to be quite expensive and frustrating for all members of the family. At the same time, Mohandas began his legal career in Bombay. He did not want to waste his London education on the backward little town of Rajkot. However, even Bombay failed to offer him the opportunities he was hoping for. He was dismayed to learn from his new colleagues that it often took several years for a barrister to earn enough of a reputation to be able to support himself. His brother Lakshmidas, who had spent a small fortune on Mohandas's education, now set about finding clients for him. When Mohandas appeared in his first court case, his "heart sank into [his] boots." He could think of no good questions to ask and thought the judge was laughing at him. Ashamed at his performance, he turned the case over to another barrister and returned to Rajkot. He was beginning to feel that the profession his brother had chosen for him was a colossal mistake.

As as a young law student (above), Mohandas dedicated himself to learning to be a proper English gentleman. He began wearing Western-style clothes and taking dance lessons.

Back in Rajkot, Mohandas set up an office and did what he considered boring and tiring work for Lakshmidas's partnership. Then one day his brother asked him to do something that sounded far more interesting. Lakshmidas had been accused of advising the ruler of Rajkot of taking some of the jewels out of the state treasury without asking permission from the British agent. Lakshmidas knew that while in London Mohandas had met Sir Edward Ollivant, the British viceroy's representative in the princely states of Rajkot and Porbandar, and asked him if he could explain the situation to him. (A *viceroy* was a colonial ruler of India, when India was a colony of the United Kingdom.) Mohandas was only too happy to oblige. When he arrived at Ollivant's office, however, he was in for a rude awakening. "Your brother is an intriguer (spy)!" Ollivant declared. "I want to hear nothing more from you." With that, the brief audience was over. Mohandas politely asked Ollivant to hear him out, but the British officer refused and had one of his servants all but throw him out. Mohandas was outraged by the way he had been treated, but there was little he could do. "This shock," he later reflected, "changed the course of my life." Obviously, speaking the Queen's English and wearing the proper attire was not enough to earn Mohandas the respect he deserved—at least not in a provincial backward place like Rajkot, where foreign dictators ruled with a heavy hand. Eager to escape this environment, Mohandas accepted the first available job that took him beyond India's borders.

## South Africa

Mohandas ended up finding a job in South Africa. Through an acquaintance of Lakshmidas's, Mohandas learned that the Indian trading firm of Dada Abdulla and Company needed a barrister to handle a "big case" there. The firm offered a salary of 105 British pounds (a living wage for a lawyer at the time), the cost of living expenses for one year, and a first-class ticket to and from the British colony of Natal. In April 1893, now 23 years old, Mohandas left his homeland for a second time. He said farewell to Kasturbai and his growing family. (Their son Manilal, their third child, was born the previous October.) Mohandas then set sail for South Africa with the promise of returning in one year.

When Mohandas arrived in the port city of Durban, he was met by his new employer, Dada Abdulla, the wealthiest Indian merchant living in the colony of Natal. (Part of the British Empire, Natal would later merge with three other British colonies to become the Union of South Africa.) A week after Mohandas's arrival in Durban, Abdulla sent him to the city of Pretoria to begin work on the case for which he had been hired. Mohandas's train stopped in Maritzburg (formally named Pietermaritzburg) around 9 o'clock that evening while traveling overnight to Pretoria. When a white boarding passenger entered his compartment and saw that Mohandas was "coloured," the passenger immediately left and returned with two officials in tow. They told Mohandas to go back to the compartment where all the "coolies" were. ("Coolie" referred to Indian laborers in South Africa. It is an insulting term.) When Mohandas refused to go to the other compartment, he was thrown off the train.

This was Mohandas's first encounter with racism, and it was a life-altering event. It was far worse than

While working as a barrister in South Africa, Mohandas (center) began to transform himself into becoming one of the leading voices of South Africa's Indian community.

the rough handling he had experienced in the office of Edward Ollivant, and his response was radically different. Instead of ignoring the *prejudice* (injustice) he had experienced or running away from it, Mohandas was determined to fight this injustice. His first step was to tell his employer, Abdulla, and write a complaint to the general manager of the railway. While Abdulla was sympathetic, the management of the railway stood by their guards and defended the way Mohandas had been treated. Mohandas was not discouraged, however, and continued to fight prejudice everywhere he found it while in South Africa. As Mohandas became involved with the men and women of Pretoria's Indian population, he began to spend much of his time and effort organizing them. He soon became a leader in the community and offered classes in the English language. Before long, Abdulla introduced Mohandas to his cousin, Tyeb Haji Khan Muhammad, a wealthy and influential merchant in Pretoria. Tyeb invited Mohandas to address the leading Indian merchants in South Africa's Transvaal colony.

In the first public speech of his life, Mohandas talked about the racial prejudice he had experienced since his arrival in South Africa. He encouraged his audience always to be honest in their business dealings, but he also urged them to forget the caste and religious differences that divided them. (Traditionally, in Indian culture, a person's *caste* (social group) determines his or her social status within the community and influences what occupations a person might hold.) These things, he said, weakened the Indian community in its struggle to gain equality and justice with South Africa's white population. In conclusion, he suggested forming an association that could bring "the hardships of the Indian settlers" to the attention of the British authorities. Mohandas made a great impression on his listeners, and the leaders of Pretoria's Indian community decided to hold weekly meetings.

> *Instead of ignoring the* prejudice *he had experienced or running away from it, Mohandas was determined to fight this injustice.*

This proved to be an incredible testing ground for Mohandas's leadership skills and launched his public career. Years later, he would refer to his early days in Pretoria as the "most valuable experience" of his life. Over the next two decades, Mohandas would call upon everything he learned during this time and transform himself into one of the leading voices of South Africa's Indian community.

By May 1894, Mohandas had resolved the legal dispute that brought him to South Africa. To show his gratitude, Abdulla hosted a farewell party for him. Mohandas, however, was not ready to leave. He had begun to lose interest in the law, but he remained eager to offer his services as adviser and spokesman of the Indian community that he had come to know so well. In the end, Mohandas had another reason to postpone his trip back home to India. A month earlier, Natal's first independent parliament had passed a discriminatory bill, and it stirred the fires of his passion for justice. Mohandas's interests at first lay primarily with the wealthy merchants who had given him so much support over the last year, but that changed quickly. He also expected to stay on just a few extra months, but this extension turned into years. During that time, something else slowly changed. Mohandas began to question the place of the Indian people in the British Empire.

# CHAPTER 2

# Civil Rights Activist

## The Natal Indian Congress

The bill that Natal's parliament passed in April 1894 was called the Franchise Law Amendment Bill. Essentially, it discriminated against Indians, denying most of them the right to vote. Mohandas was immediately aware of the bill's consequences and called it "the first nail into [the] coffin" of South Africa's Indian community. "It strikes at the root of our self-respect," he warned Dada Abdulla. Abdulla was not overly concerned about the loss of a right that he had never exercised, but he admired Mohandas and managed to secure a new job for him as a lobbyist and adviser for Natal's Indian merchant community. Mohandas wasted no time in getting to work. Using the English that he had perfected in London, he drafted a petition opposing the new bill and showed it to his new employers.

By June, Mohandas's petition was submitted to Natal's Council and Assembly along with almost 500 signatures. The petition reminded the government that the Indians living in South Africa were British subjects. As such, their rights should not be taken away. Some opponents argued that the right to vote was exclusively a European one. Calling upon his knowledge of his country's long history, Mohandas pointed out that the Indian people took part in elections long before "the Anglo-Saxon races" did. In the end, Natal's parliament passed the bill, but this came as no great surprise to Mohandas or his employers. They understood all too well the self-righteous mentality of the men they were confronting. Bracing himself for a long and difficult struggle, Mohandas

began to think of ways that he and his supporters could mobilize more effectively.

On May 22, 1894, the first meeting of what would become known as the Natal Indian Congress took place at Dada Abdulla's home. Seventy-six of Natal's wealthiest merchants were present. Most of them were Muslims, but the group also included Christians, Parsees, and a few Hindus. Mohandas served as the meeting's secretary. The Natal Indian Congress was officially founded three months later. By then it had over 200 dues-paying members. The main objective of this new association was to "promote concord and harmony among the Indians and Europeans residing in the [Natal] Colony." The Congress also intended to keep the people of Natal well informed of what its members were doing. They accomplished this by writing newspaper articles and giving lectures.

Mohandas (center, standing) poses with founders of the Natal Indian Congress, which held its first meeting in Durban, South Africa, on May 22, 1894. It was attended by Muslims, Christians, Parsees, and Hindus.

Whenever he spoke, Mohandas urged all "Colonial-born Indians" to study the history and literature of their native land. Finally, the Congress promised it would do everything possible to relieve the hardships of all Indians living in South Africa. Mohandas called for aid to be given to the "poor and helpless" to improve their "moral, social and political conditions."

During his second year of living abroad, Mohandas established a residence in one of Durban's wealthier areas overlooking the ocean. This was in keeping with his "position as an Indian barrister … and as a representative." Ironically, instead of bringing Kasturbai and his two sons to South Africa, Mohandas invited his old friend, Sheikh Mehtab, to join him and

In 1894, Natal's parliament passed a law that discriminated against Indians living in South Africa (like the ones shown below). Mohandas braced himself for a long and difficult struggle against the law.

even paid for his fare. Mohandas thought that Mehtab was clever and would make a good ally. However, their relationship soon became troubled once again. After an incident involving Mehtab and a prostitute, Mohandas was forced to distance himself. He then decided to return home, get his wife and children, and settle down in South Africa. After a six-month stay in India, Mohandas and his family sailed for Durban.

In January 1897, the SS *Courland*, the steamship that Mohandas and his family were traveling on, was detained upon reaching Durban's harbor. It remained in quarantine for five full days. The excuse given was that the officials in Durban wanted to make sure no one on board had brought the plague from India. However, Mohandas was convinced that he was the real target. By this time, he was well known for challenging racial conditions in South Africa and had made many enemies. After the quarantine finally ended, the passengers of the *Courland* were allowed to go ashore. Mohandas's suspicions were all but confirmed when a mob of angry white settlers descended upon him the moment he stepped ashore. One of them yanked off his turban. Mohandas ran for safety, but the mob chased after him, throwing rocks and rotten eggs. When he stumbled and fell, the mob began to kick him repeatedly and he lost consciousness. Mohandas's life was saved only when the wife of the police superintendent, with whom he was acquainted, came to his rescue. Following this incident,

*Mohandas urged all "Colonial-born Indians" to study the history and literature of their native land.*

Mohandas became even more famous in Durban. He used his new fame to build up the Natal Indian Congress. Over the next several years, he used the expanding organization to unite South Africa's Indian community into a powerful political force.

## The Boer War

The Gandhi family continued to grow. Shortly after Mohandas and Kasturbai settled in South Africa, their son Ramdas was born, followed by their last child, Devdas, in 1900. That same year, Mohandas became involved in the Second Boer War. The war, which had erupted the previous year, was fought between the British Empire and the Boers, also known as Afrikaners, of the Republic of Transvaal and the Orange Free State. *Boer* was a common term used to describe the white farmers living in southern Africa who descended from the original settlers sent by the Dutch East India Company. Most Indians living in South Africa viewed the Boers as a "small nation" struggling to maintain its independence in the face of obvious attempts by the British to undermine their sovereignty. Mohandas's outlook, however, was somewhat different. "We have been proud of our British citizenship," he proclaimed. "If we desire to win our freedom and achieve our welfare as members of the British Empire, here is a golden opportunity for us to do so by helping the British in the war by all the means at our disposal."

Mohandas's statement reflected his views at the time. He considered himself a faithful subject of the British Empire and was one of the most passionate

supporters of its territorial expansion during the Boer War. Mohandas was still struggling to define himself and continued to do so for many years. To strengthen his belief in the British cause, he threw himself into the war effort. In 1900, he volunteered to organize a group of Indian stretcher-bearers (medical technicians) to assist men wounded in battle. The Natal Indian Ambulance Corps had 1,100 members at its height. The Indian corps worked side by side with the European Ambulance Corps, under the direction of General Redvers Buller. Mohandas and his men served with such distinction that nearly 40 of them, including Mohandas himself, were given the Queen's South Africa Medal. "No matter how timid a man is," Mohandas later said, "he is capable of the loftiest heroism when he is put to the test."

Mohandas (front row, far right) posed with members of the Natal Indian Ambulance Corps. He formed the group of Indian medical technicians in 1900 to help men wounded during the Boer War in South Africa.

The Boer War also tested another of Mohandas's long-held beliefs. *Ahimsa*, or nonviolence, was one of the key concepts of the Hindu religion that inspired Mohandas's future career. Some of his friends thought his participation in the war effort contradicted the principles of ahimsa. Once again, Mohandas held a different view. He saw no contradiction between his Hindu faith and the actions he took during the war. He pointed out that his ambulance corps saved lives rather than ended them. In 1901, Mohandas returned to India for several months. Now 32 years old, he was impatient and eager to change the world for the better. He was also beginning to think that he should not limit his efforts to South Africa. He wanted to expand his field of service. He knew there was much to be done in his own homeland. Back in India, he immediately set to work on a resolution calling for his fellow Indians living in South Africa to be treated with justice and equality. He hoped to win the support of the Indian National Congress (INC), a broad-based political party founded in 1885. However, Mohandas's hopes for reform were dashed as he became more familiar with the Congress. Seeing its leaders up close was a disappointing experience. In describing their routine, Mohandas said they "would meet three days every year and then go to sleep." He became disillusioned with the Congress when he discovered many of its members supported caste

*"No matter how timid a man is," Mohandas later said, "he is capable of the loftiest heroism when he is put to the test."*

segregation and held a cruel prejudice against the so-called *untouchables* of Indian society. (*Untouchables* were members of India's lowest social caste.) In 1902, the Boer War ended in victory for the British as well as a further expansion of their territory in southern Africa. The Indian Ambulance Corps was disbanded well before the conclusion of hostilities, but Mohandas remained proud of his service.

After learning of the British victory over the Boers, Mohandas received a cable from a colleague in South Africa. It informed him that the British colonial secretary of state, Joseph Chamberlain, was headed to Durban to inspect the situation in South Africa personally. Dada Abdulla and others were requesting that Mohandas return immediately and use this opportunity to address the plight of South Africa's Indian community with Chamberlain. Mohandas eagerly accepted their invitation and sailed for Durban. As soon as he arrived, his friends put him to work drafting a petition for a delegation to represent the Indian community. Chamberlain, however, had come to Durban primarily to receive "a gift" of 35 million pounds from Britain's loyal subjects. With the defeat of the Boers, the white settlers had been given access to the Transvaal's plentiful gold mines, while the Indian settlers had to obtain special permits to do so. Chamberlain had little interest in the injustice suffered by the Indian population and "gave a cold shoulder" to their petition for an Indian delegation. Never easily discouraged, Mohandas was not about to give up. He continued his struggle, with renewed determination, to gain fair treatment for his fellow Indians living in South Africa.

## Fighting Prejudice and Discrimination

On June 4, 1903, Mohandas published his first newspaper, *Indian Opinion*. The paper was dedicated to the needs of Indians living in South Africa. It kept the members of the Indian community well informed on everything that affected them, good or bad. Mohandas's first editorial, however, made him sound more like an Englishman than an Indian nationalist. He referred to the "Providence" that had brought India "under the flag of Britannia," and he hailed the "great Anglo-Saxon race" and its many accomplishments. He also appealed to the Indian community to promote "harmony and good will between the different sections of the one mighty Empire." By the end of the month, Mohandas knew that he would not be finished with his work in South Africa anytime soon. Thinking it would take at least a year and perhaps several, he established a new law office in the heart of Johannesburg. He also wrote to Kasturbai in India to ask her if she would agree to remain there without him "for three or four years." During this time, Mohandas also began to read authors who would come to have a great impact on his thinking. Among them were the Americans Ralph Waldo Emerson (1803-1882) and Henry David Thoreau (1817-1862), England's John Ruskin (1819-1900), and the Russian Leo Tolstoy (1828-1910).

In July 1905, the viceroy and governor general of India, Lord Curzon, announced the *partition* (separation) of Bengal from the rest of India with the stated goal of administering the British Empire more efficiently. This partition split the largely Muslim-popu-

lated areas in the east from the largely Hindu-popu-
lated areas in the west. The Hindus of western Bengal
dominated the region's business affairs. They complained that the division would make them a minority
in the new Muslim-majority province. Indians all over
the world were outraged by this decision. They saw it
as the British Empire's attempt to "divide and rule."
The new president of the INC, Gopal Krishna Gokhale, who was to become Mohandas's political mentor,
called it a "cruel wrong." Millions of Indians were
furious over Lord Curzon's decision. They shouted
"Sva-raj!" (self-rule!) and "Freedom!"

Mass boycotts of British
goods soon erupted in Calcutta
(now known as Kolkata) and
Bombay to protest the partition.
Relenting to pressure, the
British government reunited
India and Bengal six years later,
but only after the rise of the
Indian nationalist movement.
This major change had a tremendous impact on Mohandas
as well. At the end of 1905, he
still considered himself a loyal
subject of the British Empire
and held out hope for promis-
ing reforms that would benefit
the Indian people. All of that
was about to change, however.

In March 1906, the British
declared war on the Zulu king-

In 1905, Lord Curzon
(below), the viceroy and
governor general of
India, announced the
division of Bengal from
the rest of India. This
decision enraged Indi-
ans all over the world.

dom in Natal. At first, Mohandas responded much the same way he had to the Boer War. He once again proposed an Indian Ambulance Corps during a meeting of the Natal Indian Congress in Durban. He argued that if Indians participated in the war effort, they could begin to change the prejudiced attitudes of their British rulers. Granted the rank of sergeant major, Mohandas led a corps of around 20 Indian stretcher-bearers and pledged his "true allegiance to His Majesty King Edward VII and his heirs and successors." His ambulance corps served bravely for six weeks in the summer of 1906. When the corps was disbanded in July, the Natal Indian Congress presented corps members with a medal.

*. . . every man would have to "search his own heart" and decide on the righteousness of the cause.*

Unfortunately, the prejudice that Indians experienced in South Africa only seemed to intensify after the Zulu rebellion of 1906. In response, the Natal Indian Congress sent Mohandas to London as part of a delegation to lobby on behalf of South Africa's Indian community. When he arrived in the British capital, Mohandas had his first encounter with Winston Churchill. Churchill, who was colonial undersecretary of state at the time, attempted to justify the "deprivation of the franchise from British Indians." He argued that all "non-European natives" were "coloured people" and therefore incapable of self-government. This marked the beginning of a long-standing and bitter feud between Mohandas and Churchill. The feud would endure—and intensify—over the next 40 years.

## Satyagraha (Nonviolent Resistance)

Shortly after Mohandas's return to South Africa, the Legislative Council of the Transvaal introduced the Transvaal Asiatic Registration Act. It required all Indians, including women and children, to register with the government, be fingerprinted, and carry identification cards with them wherever they went. For Mohandas, this type of discrimination was a step too far. Writing an editorial in the *Indian Opinion*, he called the proposed law "abominable" and "criminal." In September 1906, he organized a mass rally at Johannesburg's Empire Theatre. Nearly 3,000 Indians attended. During his speech, Mohandas urged his listeners to take an oath against the government, which, he said, had "taken leave of all sense of decency." Not to oppose the government's "tyrannical" new law would be considered "cowardice." But he admitted that every man would have to "search his own heart" and decide on the righteousness of the cause. This was the beginning of Mohandas's revolutionary method of nonviolent or passive resistance, which he referred to as *Satyagraha* (pronounced *SUHT yuh GRUH huh*). Loosely translated from Sanskrit, Satyagraha means "holding fast to the truth." Mohandas found inspiration for his gradually expanding beliefs in a letter that Leo Tolstoy wrote to Tarak Nath Das, a Bengali Indian scholar and revolutionary. Mohandas urged all Indians living in South Africa to ignore the new law and be willing to suffer the consequences. Unfortunately, the Legislative Council of the Transvaal was not moved by Mohandas's speech.

# Indian Opinion

PUBLISHED WEEKLY IN ENGLISH AND GUJARATI

No. 45—Vol. XI. Wednesday, November 12th, 1913.

## A WEEK OF EXCITEMENT

THE week which ended on the 8th instant will long be remembered as one of tremendous moment to the Indian community of South Africa. Each day there was reported the rapid development of the strike movement, and when, on Friday last, the news came to hand that Mr. Gandhi had been arrested, things seemed to have developed into a crisis. From the reports we have received ourselves and the summaries by Reuter and other correspondents, we give as complete a review of the happenings of the week as it is possible in the space and time at our disposal.

**Mohandas wrote an editorial in his weekly newspaper, *Indian Opinion* (above), to help prepare the Indian community to resist what he called the discriminatory "Black Act" of 1907.**

Mohandas wrote another editorial for the *Indian Opinion* to help prepare the Indian community to resist the so-called "Black Act" when it went into effect on January 1, 1907. The editorial detailed the lives of many brave people throughout the history of the British Empire who had challenged *tyranny*, or the unjust use of power, and oppression. Through their suffering, each of them had won their freedom in the end. The implied promise, of course, was that if enough Indians living in South Africa were willing to fight this unjust law by going to jail, they would receive the same reward in their struggle. Mohandas also made another trip to England as part of a delegation that pleaded their case before the colonial secretary of state, Lord Elgin. By the time he returned to South Africa, however, Mohandas was firmly convinced that "salvation" lay not with the British but in the hands of the Indian people. On New Year's Day, he addressed the Natal Indian Congress in Durban and proclaimed, "Our struggle has just begun."

The first Indian to be prosecuted for disobeying the new law was a Hindu man named Ram Sundar Pundit. Mohandas immediately offered to represent him in court as his lawyer. However, he offered no defense since his client readily admitted that he lacked the proper papers and did not wish to post bail, even though many of his fellow Indians offered to bail him out of jail. Mohandas himself was arrested for not having the proper "registration certificate." He was first tried on December 28, 1907, and found guilty. He was given 48 hours to leave the Transvaal colony. Refusing to do so, he was called back to court in January 1908, charged with contempt of court, and sentenced to two months in prison. His first experience with imprisonment affected Mohandas much more deeply than he could have imagined, but he became convinced of the power of Satyagraha. "I seem to hear it whispered in my ear that God is always the friend and protector of truth," he wrote at the time. "Our success in bringing this campaign to this stage is a triumph of truth."

*His first experience with imprisonment affected Mohandas much more deeply than he could have imagined . . .*

On January 30, after more than two weeks in jail, Mohandas was taken by the superintendent of police to meet with General Jan Smuts. Smuts, who eventually became South Africa's second prime minister, had a formidable mind for the law and proved to be one of Mohandas's most brilliant opponents. On behalf of the government, Smuts offered to withdraw the forced registration of all Indians living in the Transvaal colony. This part of the law had so angered the Indian community and was the main source of conflict. In return, Mohandas would have to convince his fellow Indians to register voluntarily "and not under any law." Believing Smuts to be sincere, Mohandas agreed to his terms and was set free. Upon his return to Johannesburg, he told his friends about the "victory" he had won. Surprised to find that Mohandas was no longer in prison, many of them did not think General Smuts could be taken at his word. They did not see it as a victory at all. Some even suspected Mohandas of plotting with Smuts. As he had promised the general, Mohandas went to the permit office to be the first to register voluntarily. However, a Pashtun man knocked him to the ground and beat him severely. This was the first—but not the last—time that some of Mohandas's followers doubted his honesty.

Three months later, General Smuts went back on his word. He announced that all Indians who had failed to register voluntarily would be forced to do so or be expelled from the colony. The betrayal that Mohandas felt was keen. Once again, the government started sending Indians to jail in droves. Mohandas represented many of them and never pleaded for mercy. Among those imprisoned was his son, Harilal. By mid-August 1908, with more than 60 Indians sitting in Johannesburg's jails, Mohandas wrote General Smuts and once again requested him to repeal the "Black Act." After receiving no answer from General Smuts, Mohandas spoke at a meeting of the Indian community and urged all those assembled to burn their identification certificates. By the end of the month, 2,300 Indians had burned their certificates. Mohandas was imprisoned more than once over the next several months.

In February 1909, Mohandas received a three-month sentence, but he remained cheerful. Quoting

Mohandas recuperates from injuries he suffered when a Pashtun man knocked him to the ground and beat him severely. It was the first time one of his followers had doubted his honesty.

Thoreau, he said that prison was the only appropriate place for a free man to live in an unjust state. Mohandas devoted himself regularly to prayers while in jail. Upon his release in May, he was hailed in Johannesburg as "King of the Hindus and Muslims." He was overcome with emotion. But Mohandas did not accept the honor. "I am a servant of the community," he replied, "not its king. I pray to God to grant me the strength … to lay down my life in the very act of serving."

Mohandas had gone through an internal transformation over the last 18 months. It was obvious to all those who knew him. The British barrister who had been placed in iron cuffs now emerged as the passionate leader of the Indian community. He was well on his way to becoming the Mahatma, worshipped by millions of his countrymen. By this time, Mohandas had also told Kasturbai that he intended to take a vow of *chastity* (moral purity; virtue; giving up sexual activity) to conserve his creative energy and to channel it into what he now considered a spiritual battle. According to Hindu religious tradition, a man who has come of age and fathered a son to carry on the family name may take such a vow. This is known as *brahmacharya*. Kasturbai understood this to be a serious and lifelong commitment.

The key to his own personal transformation had been the power of Satyagraha, and Mohandas understood that it would be the key to transforming the Indian people as well. After he was released from prison in May 1909, he clearly expressed his spiritually inspired method of nonviolent resistance. "If we learn the use of the weapon of the Satyagraha," he said, "we can employ it to overcome all hardships originating from injustice." His specific grievance was against the "Black Act" that affected the relatively small Indian community in the Natal and Transvaal colonies. It was now a message that would echo beyond the borders of South Africa.

## "Purifying Suffering"

In July 1909, Mohandas made yet another trip to London as part of an Indian delegation. During his stay in the British capital, he continued to demand justice and equality for the Indians living in South

Africa. He swore he would never give up this struggle for as long as he lived. Nevertheless, Mohandas was usually disappointed after his repeated meetings with London's government officials, and this was beginning to wear on him. "I have grown disillusioned with Western civilization," he said. This view, along with his dislike of the pollution and violence of large cities, would remain with him for the rest of his life.

When Mohandas's delegation left London in November 1909, his thinking became clearer. He sat down and wrote his first major book, *Hind Swaraj* (*Indian Home Rule*), during the two weeks or so that he spent on the high seas on his way back to South Africa. The book was written in Gujarati, his native language, and it was published in two separate issues of the *Indian Opinion*. The book was translated into English in 1910. Mohandas wrote *Hind Swaraj* in the form of a dialogue, the same structure of many ancient Indian philosophical works. Receiving praise from many circles, he humbly attributed his inspiration to Leo Tolstoy's book, *The Kingdom of God Is Within You*. Mohandas's critique of Britain's rule over the subcontinent attracted the attention of the British authorities in India. They quickly censored his book.

*Mohandas's critique of Britain's rule over the subcontinent attracted the attention of the British authorities in India.*

On June 1, 1910, the four British colonies of Natal, the Transvaal, the Orange River Colony (formerly the Orange Free State), and the Cape of Good Hope merged to form the Union of South Africa. Louis

Botha was elected its first prime minister, but Jan Smuts, the principal architect of the Union, remained its dominant political force. In March 1911, Smuts oversaw the passage of a new bill intended to repeal the "Black Act" of 1907. At first, Mohandas was hopeful that the new bill would provide the justice for the Indian community that he had long sought. However, most of the whites in South Africa maintained their prejudice against the Indian population. When Smuts's Asiatic Immigration Bill went through South Africa's parliament the following year, it reflected this unfair prejudice. Upon reading the final version,

Indian nationalist leader Gopal Krishna Gokhale (center, wearing long scarf) traveled to South Africa in late 1912 to support Mohandas's plan to launch a new protest movement.

Mohandas was dismayed by its harsh measures and called it the "Asiatic Expulsion Bill." He warned the Indian community that a "still greater purifying suffering" would be needed, and he immediately prepared himself for a renewal of Satyagraha. Mohandas kept his mentor, the Indian nationalist leader Gopal Krishna Gokhale, informed of his plan to launch a new protest movement. Gokhale made a trip to South Africa in late 1912 to support his protégé. The battle lines were drawn the following summer.

By October 1913, nearly 100 Indians had been put in jail for defying the new law. Mohandas himself was arrested on November 7 and charged with aiding "prohibited persons" from entering the Transvaal. Released on bail, he wasted no time in joining the "Great March" that was taking place near Prime Minister Botha's farm. When the protesters saw Mohandas, they cheered him and hailed him as *Bapu* (a Gujarati term of affection meaning "father" or "papa"). Several Indians were killed by white soldiers during the march. The soldiers later claimed they had acted in self-defense. After this, Mohandas stopped dressing in the suits he had worn as a barrister over the last 20 years. Instead, he donned the simple clothing of an indentured laborer and started shaving his head. He would never again wear Western-style clothing. Mohandas's process of "purification" was now complete.

General Smuts offered to meet with Mohandas to avoid further bloodshed. On Jan. 9, 1914, Mohandas traveled to Pretoria to meet with him. Smuts was "patient and conciliatory" during the meeting. He had developed a grudging respect for Mohandas and his "unusual humanity" over the years. By the end of the month, the two men had reached a "provisional agreement" on all points of dispute. The temporary deal abolished a law passed the year before that recognized only Christian marriages as legal, and it once again allowed Indians born in South Africa to travel freely between the Cape of Good Hope and the Orange River Colony. Mohandas returned to Durban to inform his colleagues about the agreement. It was unanimously endorsed. He was proud of the success he had achieved.

Mohandas felt that he had done everything he could to help South Africa's Indian community. He was eager to return to India and spend some time in spiritual retreat with his mentor, Gokhale, in the city of Poona (now known as Pune). The summer of 1914 found Gokhale in London, however, so Mohandas traveled there first to connect with him. On July 18, he and Kasturbai sailed for England. When the couple arrived, they learned that the British Empire was once again at war. This conflict, first known as the Great War and now known as World War I, would preoccupy the British government—and the world—for the next four years. Those years would also witness the beginning of the greatest struggle of Mohandas's life.

# CHAPTER 3

# The Struggle for Independence

## Return to India

Like most people in London, Mohandas was hopeful that the Great War would be over by the end of the year. He once again offered to raise an Indian Ambulance Corps to support British troops on the battlefront in France. During his first six weeks in London, Mohandas took nursing classes. He spent as much time as possible taking care of his ailing mentor, Gokhale, who was suffering from a bad case of diabetes. Mohandas's own health concerns kept him from the front lines, and Colonel R. J. Baker was appointed to take charge of the Indian medical corps. By the end of October, Mohandas's health condition had grown worse. He was coughing up blood and restricted to bed for two weeks. During his recuperation, he told his friends that he was tired of being in London. "My soul is in India," he said.

In early December 1914, Mohandas was still confined to bed. He was quite thin and weak. At 45 years of age, he was starting to fear the worst. Fortunately, keeping to a diet of banana biscuits and dried fruit soaked in water, his health slowly improved. By the end of the month, he was feeling well enough to attend a farewell dinner given for him and Kasturbai at the Westminster Palace Hotel. He was at last returning to India, where he hoped to regain his strength. On January 9, 1915, Mohandas and his wife arrived in Bombay aboard the SS *Arabia*. They were "exceedingly glad to see … the dear old Motherland." In February, Mohandas went to Poona to see Gokhale, who had returned to India ahead of him. He visited the Servants of India Society, an organization that

Gokhale had founded to advance Indian education. Mohandas was greatly impressed with the work his friend had done. The two men enjoyed their brief time together. Unfortunately, it would be their last opportunity. Gokhale passed away less than a week after Mohandas's visit. Mohandas was greatly saddened upon hearing the news of his mentor's death.

Mohandas returned to Poona a month later, hoping to live at the Servants of India Society and take up Gokhale's mantle of leadership. However, many of the society's members were fearful of his radical ideas. Instead of greeting him with open arms, they drove him away from Poona. Mohandas later established his own *ashram*, or religious retreat, on the outskirts of Ahmedabad, the city where he had graduated from high school. Calling it the Satyagraha Ashram, he founded it on May 20, 1915. He drafted a constitution

Mohandas (in white turban) received a hero's welcome upon his return to India in 1915 for his work in South Africa. He was invited to speak at the convention of the Indian National Congress.

for the ashram. It required all of its members to take vows of truth, nonviolence, celibacy, control of the palate (appetite), and refrain from stealing and owning any possessions. By November, Mohandas had enlisted 33 residents to live and work at his busy ashram. When he admitted his first untouchable family, Kasturbai became so upset that she threatened to leave him. However, Mohandas was determined to challenge injustice wherever he found it, even in the foundation of Indian society.

Following the advice of his late mentor, Mohandas traveled across India over the next several years getting to know his home country again. He gave speeches everywhere he went. He condemned "all acts of violence" and stressed the need to secure "the utmost freedom" for his country. He unveiled portraits and statues of Gokhale, addressed Gujarati merchant societies, and formally opened schools. One of the schools he visited was founded and run by the Bengali poet Rabindranath Tagore. It was during his visit with Tagore that Mohandas was first addressed by anyone as *Mahatma*, or Great Soul. Mohandas also became involved in India's political arena. In 1915, he joined the Indian National Congress and became absorbed with the issues affecting the Indian people. He frequently appeared at gatherings of the Muslim League as well. The following year, he attended the annual Bombay Provincial Conference, where he supported Muhammad Ali Jinnah as its president.

> *He drafted a constitution for the ashram. It required all of its members to take vows of truth . . .*

Mohandas set up this religious retreat (left), which he called the Satyagraha Ashram, on the outskirts of Ahmedabad, the city where he had graduated from high school.

(Years later, Jinnah would become the founder of the modern state of Pakistan.) When he was not traveling or speaking to crowds, Mohandas spent most of his time at his ashram.

## Effects of World War I

In April 1918, toward the end of World War I, Lord Chelmsford, who had become viceroy of India two years earlier, invited Mohandas to address a military conference in the city of Delhi. In a surprising turn of events, Mohandas agreed to start recruiting for the British war effort. This time Mohandas joined in the recruitment of combatants, in contrast to his response to the Zulu rebellion of 1906. In June of that year, he wrote a pamphlet titled "Appeal for Enlistment." He stated that all men "should have the ability to defend" themselves. He stressed in a letter to Lord Chelmsford's personal secretary, John Maffey, that he would not personally "kill or injure anybody, friend or foe."

Mohandas followed through on his recruitment campaign with complete commitment, as he did with everything else in his life. For several months, he thought and spoke about little else. Mohandas referred to his own state of mind as "recruiting madness." However, his support of the British war effort made some of his followers once again doubt his sincerity. They thought his actions violated the principles of ahimsa. Mahadev Desai, a young man who was Mohandas's personal secretary, noted that even some of his closest associates found this decision perplexing. Desai would faithfully serve as Mohandas' personal secretary for a quarter century.

*. . . civil disobedience was "a duty imposed upon every lover of personal and public liberty."*

When World War I ended in November 1918, Mohandas naturally expected India to be rewarded for its support of the British war effort both in men and military equipment. There had been hints that India would be granted dominion (self-governing) status after the war. Instead, the viceroy's legislative council enforced martial law throughout India, even though every Indian representative serving on the council objected to the decision. For Mohandas, the long-term impact of World War I was his belated recognition of what he called Britain's "determined policy of repression" in India. In response, he said that civil disobedience was "a duty imposed upon every lover of personal and public liberty." Mohandas braced himself for a struggle to obtain Indian home rule. But he had no idea it would consume the next 30 years of his life.

## Political Agitation

Mohandas was now convinced that the time had come to launch a Satyagraha movement in his homeland. The question was where to begin. He decided on Champaran, a region in northeastern India, when he became aware of the terrible exploitation of tenant farmers taking place there. The people of Champaran grew indigo, a cash crop whose value was in slow and steady decline. (*Indigo* is a plant from which a deep blue dye was made.) At the urging of the British landlords in Champaran, the local government forced the workers to sell their crops at a fixed price. Mohandas, along with a hand-picked team of prominent lawyers, organized a survey of Champaran's villages. They detailed the incredible suffering that had taken place there, including its general state of impoverished living. Once Mohandas had gained the confidence of the locals, he and his followers began to clean up their villages, building schools and hospitals. At the same time, Mohandas led a nonviolent protest that challenged the British landlords' attempt to keep the people of Champaran in poverty. He was joined in his efforts by many young Indian nationalists from all over the country.

The British authorities responded by arresting Mohandas and charging him with inciting civil unrest. Thousands of people rallied to his defense. His supporters gathered outside the jail where he was detained, demanding that he be released. The courts did so reluctantly, but only after Mohandas obtained an agreement that guaranteed improved compensation for the indigo workers and gave them greater control over their farming practices. After this victory, Mohandas was ordered by the courts to leave the province. He then moved on to Kheda, a district in India's northwest corner. Kheda was experiencing flooding and famine conditions, and the residents were requesting the government to suspend their taxes for one year. When the residents received only partial relief from the government, Mohandas appealed to the governor in Bombay to suspend the collection of taxes for the entire district. He warned the British commissioner of his intentions to visit Kheda and proposed a meeting with his representative. After failing to arrange a meeting, Mohandas declared Satyagraha at a gathering of some 5,200 people in the city of Nadiad. He proposed that the people of Kheda pursue a policy of noncooperation. He said they should refuse to pay taxes to the government, even if they were threatened with seizure of their land. Mohandas worked hard to win the support of the public. For several months, the government refused to negotiate. But eventually it agreed to provide tax relief to the people of Kheda until the famine was over.

Around this time, Mohandas began making appeals to India's Muslim community. Disputes between Hindus and Muslims were a common occurrence in India. But Mohandas sought political cooperation from both sides to end British domination of their common homeland. He joined pan-Islamic leaders whenever possible. In Delhi, Mohandas spoke to a large Muslim audience at the Khilafat Conference. The purpose of the conference was to protest the breakup of the Ottoman Empire by the Allies, despite Britain and France's promises not to do so. (The Ottomans, which had supported Germany, were defeated by the Allies in World War I.) Most Muslims considered the ruler of the Ottoman Empire, known as the caliph, as a symbol of solidarity for the world-wide Islamic community and did not want to see the office of the caliphate abolished. By allying himself with the Khilafat movement, Mohandas gained strong support among India's Muslim population, but it also created problems. Several promi-nent Hindus—including Rabin-dranath Tagore, who won the Nobel Prize in literature in 1913—began to question Mohan-das's leadership and dedication to his own religion.

Mohandas's support of the Ottoman caliph ended the open hostility—at least temporarily—between India's Hindu and Muslim communities and united them in a common cause against their British overlords. It also helped to silence the criticism of the Indian Muslim leader Mu-hammad Ali Jinnah, who op-posed Mohandas's policy of Satyagraha. In 1924, the caliph-ate was formally abolished by the Republic of Turkey, which was created out of the Ottoman

Mohandas is shown here after launching his first campaign of Satyagraha (nonviolent or passive resistence) against British repres-sion in India.

Empire. By then, the Khilafat movement had ended. With its dissolution, most of India's Muslims abandoned their support for Mohandas and the Indian National Congress, and the conflict between Hindus and Muslims resumed. However, Mohandas's temporary alliance with the Khilafat movement raised his standing as a political leader in the eyes of the British.

## Noncooperation and Massacre

On February 24, 1919, Mohandas wrote to the viceroy of India, Lord Chelmsford, and asked him to reconsider his decision to enforce the Rowlatt Bills. Also known as the "Black Act" or "Black Bills," the Rowlatt Bills extended the Defense of India Act, officially announced in 1915, that established martial law in India. The bills would make organizing opposition to the government against the law. If enacted, Mohandas promised to launch another campaign of Satyagraha. He proposed that his followers "commit civil disobedience of such laws" and pursue a strategy of noncooperation. The following day, 50 of them signed a pledge to do so. Around the same time, Mohandas started Satyagraha Sabha, a new committee to help him recruit volunteers to launch an effective civil disobedience protest.

On March 30, police in Delhi opened fire on a crowd of peaceful demonstrators protesting the enactment of the "Black Bills." Many were killed, and riots followed. Mohandas proclaimed April 6 as a day of national mourning and spent the day in Bombay, praying and fasting. He also reminded his followers never to respond with violence. Instead, he suggested a boycott of British goods, encouraging his supporters to burn all British clothing that they might own. Mohandas's faith in his campaign of Satyagraha grew as it gained momentum. Cities and villages across India protested in defiance of British laws. On April 8, he took the train from Bombay to Delhi. The following day, however, the government served him with an order not to enter the city. He ignored the warning and attempted to enter Delhi. He was promptly arrested and forced to return to Bombay under police guard. When the public heard the news, more riots followed. Crowds in Bombay threw rocks at governmental buildings and obstructed traffic. As soon as Mohandas learned of the violence, he strongly scolded his followers. "This is not Satyagraha," he said. "If we cannot conduct this movement without the slightest violence from our side, the movement might have to be abandoned."

Several days later, a large crowd of people, many of them women and children, gathered in Amritsar, in the province of Punjab in northern India. There was also a large group of religious pilgrims in the city. They chose the Jallianwala Bagh public garden for their protest. Jallianwala Bagh was a large open area nearly seven acres in size. On the morning of April 13, Brigadier General Reginald Dyer, the acting commander of the city's military garrison, issued a proclamation announcing that passes would now be required both to enter and leave Amritsar. Starting that evening, a curfew was put into effect, and public gatherings that consisted of four or more people were banned. Dyer, like many officers of the British army stationed in India, thought that a revolt by the native population was becoming more and more likely.

Thousands of Hindus, Muslims, and Sikhs (Sikhism is another world religion that originated in India) assembled to peacefully protest the "Black Bills," as planned, despite Dyer's proclamation. An hour after the protest began, General Dyer showed up with 90 soldiers armed with rifles. He also brought two armored cars that carried machine guns. Dyer had the main entrances of Jallianwala Bagh blocked. Without warning the crowd to disperse, he ordered his troops to fire at the protesters. The soldiers, taking aim with their rifles, shot into the densest part of the crowd for about 10 minutes. Dyer told his men to stop only when their supply of ammunition was nearly exhausted. Nearly 1,650 rounds had been spent. Many people attempting to escape the slaughter were crushed to death in the stampede that followed. Hundreds of people were killed and well over 1,000 were wounded. Dyer's troops withdrew without providing medical assistance or giving any thought to those who had been injured. It was the worst massacre in India's history.

*He suspended his calls for civil disobedience and went on a fast, vowing not to eat again until the rioting had ended.*

The British government immediately tried to suppress any information about the massacre from getting out by declaring martial law in Punjab province. For this reason, details about the massacre were slow to spread across India. When Mohandas learned of the massacre the following day, he did not criticize the British for their actions. Instead, he lashed out at his fellow countrymen for the violence that was rocking India. Mohandas said that he was "ashamed" by their behavior. He demanded that his followers refrain from all violent acts and stop the widespread destruction of property that was taking place. He suspended his calls for civil disobedience and went on a fast, vowing not to eat again until the rioting had ended.

It was not until the end of 1919 that Mohandas—and the rest of the world—became aware of the full magnitude of the horrible crime committed in Amritsar. When details of the massacre became widely known that December, the British Prime Minister H. H. Asquith called the attack "one of the worst outrages in the whole of [British] history." Winston Churchill, now secretary of state for war, openly condemned Dyer's brutality in the House of Commons. Nevertheless, General Dyer, who claimed he was "confronted by a revolutionary army," did not receive any serious disciplinary action and was permitted to resign. Many Indians felt the "Butcher of Amritsar," as Dyer later became known, had gotten away with murder. Mohandas became convinced that the British would never give the people of India fair and equal treatment. He felt that the only way forward was for them to take control of their own destiny.

## Victories and Setbacks

After the massacre in Amritsar, Mohandas focused all his energies on achieving self-rule for India. In December 1919, nearly 15,000 people attended the meeting of the Indian National Congress that took place in

Amritsar. During the meeting, Mohandas was invited to serve on a committee to rewrite the constitution of the INC. He gladly accepted. He hoped it would give him the opportunity to transform the mostly moderate organization into a truly national and revolutionary party that would achieve home rule for India. He was also elected president of the India Home Rule League, which he later merged with the INC.

In July 1920, Mohandas, with the power and influence of a reorganized INC behind him, announced his intentions of launching another Satyagraha campaign. He was determined to expand his political and economic strategy against the British Empire as well. One way to do this was to promote the principle of *swadeshi* (self-sufficiency), which called for the *boycott* of foreign businesses and products. (Boycott means to join together against and having nothing to do with a person, business, or nation as a punishment or to force a change in policy or behavior.) Mohandas suggested that Indian men and women, rich and poor alike, spend a little time each day spinning *khadi*, a type of homespun cloth, in support of Indian independence. Around this time, Mohandas, desiring to identify with India's poor, began wearing only a white *dhoti* (loincloth) and a shawl. He also encouraged his followers to boycott all British institutions in India, such as law courts, and to resign from government jobs. On August 1, Mohandas met with the viceroy of India and

> *Mohandas, desiring to identify with India's poor, began wearing only a white dhoti (loincloth) and a shawl.*

returned the medals he had won for his work in South Africa. By now, wherever he went in India, he was greeted by crowds who shouted, "Victory to Mahatma Gandhi!"

Mohandas's call for noncooperation became more harsh and insistent, and it resounded with the people of India. Many young radicals joined his movement during this time. Among them was Jawaharlal Nehru. Nehru would become one of Mohandas's greatest allies, eventually helping to win India's independence and serving as the country's first prime minister. As the passionate enthusiasm of his followers increased, Mohandas became aware of the pitfalls that came with his growing political power. He even began to fear it. "We are in sight of the Promised Land," he told his followers, "but the danger is the greatest when victory seems the nearest." Once again, Mohandas reminded them that nonviolence was the "most vital and integral part" of noncooperation. Even so, his warnings were not taken to heart by many of his followers, and episodes of terrible violence continued. One of the worst took place in February 1922 in Chauri Chaura when a large group of protesters clashed with police, who then opened fire on them. In retaliation, the protesters set fire to a police station,

Jawaharlal Nehru (above as a young radical) joined Mohandas's Indian independence movement and became one of his greatest allies. Nehru later became India's prime minister.

killing more than 20 officers. When his son Devdas told him what had happened, Mohandas was shattered by the news. He condemned the "inhuman conduct" of Chauri Chaura's murderous mob. Mohandas assumed full responsibility for the crime. He ended his Satyagraha campaign and called for all further civil disobedience to be suspended. On March 18, 1922, the British government arrested Mohandas for *sedition* (causing a rebellion). He was put on trial and given a six-year sentence, which was to be served in the massive Yeravada Prison in Poona.

While in prison, Mohandas had ample time to reflect on the errors he had made. He felt that he had misled many of his followers into thinking that they could win India's freedom overnight. He took a vow of silence and spent his time spinning cotton thread. He

Around 1920, Mohandas (below) began wearing only a white *dhoti* (loincloth traditionally worn by Hindu men), sometimes with a shawl, to identify with the poor people of India.

considered his *charkha*, or spinning wheel, as the only thing capable of making Indians feel as if they were all "children of the same land." Eating just minimal portions of food twice a day, Mohandas's weight dropped to 99 pounds (45 kilograms). His actions soon endangered his health. A life-saving operation became necessary in January 1924. Afterward, the viceroy of India released Mohandas from prison with "considerations of his health" in mind, and Mohandas returned to his ashram.

Mohandas began another tour of India the following year. Everywhere he went, he attempted to reunite the various factions that seemed to have moved further apart during his time in prison. Once again, he focused on relations between Hindus and Muslims. Ever since the Khilafat movement died out, there had been little political cooperation between the two groups. Eventually, Mohandas found the issue of Hindu-Muslim unity to be a "hopeless tangle." Turning back to his Hindu roots, Mohandas rededicated himself to the religion of his birth. He did so not only for the natural comfort that it provided, but also to address some of its darker practices such as the notion of "untouchability." He considered it be to "a blot upon humanity and therefore upon Hinduism."

Around this time, Mohandas began to attract the attention of the world press, and many journalists came to visit him at his ashram. An Indian correspondent living in London asked Mohandas what India could contribute toward world peace. Mohandas responded, "If India succeeds in regaining her liberty through nonviolent means, she would have made the largest contribution yet known to world peace." An American reporter challenged Mohandas's message of nonviolence, saying that "the average person is not a Mahatma." Mohandas replied, "I am as frail a mortal as any of us and … liable to err like any other fellow mortal. I own, however, that I have humility enough in me to confess my errors and to retrace my steps." Over the next several years, Mohandas concerned himself mostly with spinning cloth, taking care of his health, and attending to his ashram "family." However, he had not lost hope in his dream of self-rule for India. In time, Mohandas regained his faith to inspire his followers to achieve that goal through nonviolent means. Before long, he was ready for the next big push.

## The Salt March

In December 1928, Mohandas urged the Indian National Congress to pass a resolution concerning India's place in the British Empire. It called for the British government to grant India *dominion* (self-governing) status or face a new wave of noncooperation. The Congress passed the resolution, but the British government failed to respond as Mohandas had hoped. In January the following year, he began to remobilize his movement and quickly regained its lost momentum. He organized committees to gather volunteers to go from door to door in every town and village to initiate a new boycott. "Picketing foreign cloth shops may be undertaken wherever possible," he told his supporters. Many believed that this Satyagraha campaign would be the final push toward achieving national independence. Mohandas confirmed as much during an interview later in 1929. When a reporter asked how this campaign would be different from the one launched eight years earlier, Mohandas stated clearly that the goal this time was "complete independence."

On December 31, Mohandas, Jawaharlal Nehru, and other members of the INC gathered in the city of Lahore (a city within India's borders at that time but today the second largest city in Pakistan) and issued a proclamation declaring India's sovereignty and self-rule. "We believe that it is the inalienable right of the Indian people," Nehru said, "to have freedom and to enjoy the fruits of their toil. … We believe therefore, that India must sever the British connection and attain *Purna Swaraj* or complete sovereignty and self-rule." The tricolor banner of India was unfurled and raised for the first time. Nehru added that the "national flag of Hindustan" would proudly wave "so long as a single Indian … lives in India." People across the country celebrated this revolutionary action as 1930 was ushered in. The INC declared January 26 to be Purna Swaraj Day. It has been observed as the country's Independence Day ever since.

The INC then assigned Mohandas the task of launching a new wave of civil disobedience. His plan was to begin a major campaign of Satyagraha against the British salt tax, which he felt was the most unjust of all. The Salt Act of 1882 had given the British government a monopoly on the collection and manufacture of

> *"We believe that it is the inalienable right of the Indian people to have freedom and to enjoy the fruits of their toil."*

**Indian freedom fighter and poet Sarojini Naidu (right) marched with Mohandas and his followers during the 240-mile Salt March in 1930 to boycott the British tax on salt in India.**

salt in India and imposed a substantial tax. The tax represented more than 8 percent of the annual tax revenue collected from the Indian people. Though salt could easily be obtained through evaporation of seawater and was freely available to people living along India's extensive coastline, the country's inhabitants were compelled to buy it through the government. Violation of the Salt Act was considered a criminal offense punishable by imprisonment. When Mohandas announced his idea of boycotting salt to the INC, its leadership thought it was a poor decision. When the British government learned of the planned resistance to the salt tax, they did not take it seriously either. Mohandas argued that opposing the salt tax was a deeply symbolic choice. Salt was used by nearly everyone in India. "Next to air and water," he explained, "salt is perhaps the greatest necessity of life." He felt that boycotting the British tax on salt would underscore the INC's declaration of Purna Swaraj. It would give it real meaning to the men and women of India, especially the poor, for whom salt was the only *condiment* (seasoning) they could afford. Mohandas felt that bringing the poor into the struggle for India's sovereignty would be necessary to achieve victory. He also pointed out that this was something that both Hindus and Muslims, despite their many differences, would be able to support. Eventually, Mohandas won the support of the Congress and proceeded with his plan.

On February 5, 1930, the press reported Mohandas's plan to boycott the British tax on salt. His campaign of Satyagraha would begin on March 12 and end in the village of Dandi on the coast of the Arabian Sea. The plan was to arrive there on April 5. The Salt March, as it came to be known, would last 24 days; it would pass through four districts and nearly 50 villages. Ten days before beginning the march, Mohandas wrote to Lord Irwin, who had become viceroy of India in 1926, and informed him of his plans. Mohandas said he was willing to seek a way out "before embarking on civil disobedience and taking the risk I have dreaded to take all these years." Irwin refused to meet with Mohandas in person. He said that he "regretted" Mohandas's decision, which would "involve violation of the law and danger to the public peace." Thus began Mohandas's hardest and most difficult struggle against the world's largest and most powerful empire.

Mohandas kept the press well informed of his plans by issuing regular statements from his ashram in the days leading up to the Salt March. "We are entering upon a life and death struggle, a holy war," he said. "We are performing an all-embracing sacrifice." During the march, Mohandas told all those who went with him that he expected them to firmly heed his strict rules of nonviolence. The group included members of the INC as well as residents of his ashram.

When March 12 dawned, Mohandas and 80 of his supporters set out on foot from Sabarmati Ashram, near Ahmadabad, for the Arabian Sea village of Dandi, about 240 miles away. According to *The Statesman*, India's official government newspaper, a crowd of nearly 100,000 people gathered to witness the event.

The first day ended in the village of Aslali. There, Mohandas spoke to a crowd of about 4,000 people. He talked about the "poor man's struggle" in India and the burdensome salt tax imposed by the British. At the end of every day, Mohandas expected to be arrested, but much to his disappointment he was not arrested. At every stop in villages along the way, donations were collected and new supporters were recruited. Mohandas also sent scouts ahead to the next village so that he could address the issues of the people to whom he spoke. The marchers spent each night sleeping in the open, with the press continuing to report on all their activities. By the time Mohandas and his followers, who by then had swelled into the hundreds, reached their destination, the press had turned Gandhi into a household name across the world.

On April 5, speaking to reporters in Dandi, Mohandas said, "God be thanked for what may be termed the happy ending of the first stage in this, for me at least, the final struggle for freedom. ... I expect my companions to commence actual civil disobedience at 6:30 tomorrow morning." The following day, holding up a handful of salt-rich soil, he declared, "With this, I am shaking the foundations of the British Empire." He then urged his thousands of followers to begin producing salt from the sea. Civil disobedience spread throughout India as millions opposed the Salt Act and illegally produced salt along India's coasts, where it was then sold. In response, the British government arrested over 60,000 people by the end of April.

The Satyagraha of the Salt March quickly became a mass movement that spread across India. More British goods were boycotted and other unpopular laws were challenged. In turn, the British responded by enforcing new laws, declaring the INC and other organizations to be illegal. None of these measures worked, however, and violence erupted in Calcutta and Karachi. But this time Mohandas calmly urged his followers to respond to the British unjust use of power with nonviolence. The British government was shaken by the effects of the Salt March. Officials were torn about whether to arrest Mohandas but were

Mohandas (left, wearing a shawl) and thousands of his followers collect salt from the sea shore to begin producing salt in violation of the British Salt Act. Over 60,000 people were arrested.

determined not to make a *martyr* of him. (A martyr is a person who suffers, or chooses to die, for a particular belief.) Eventually, the British decided that taking Mohandas into custody was the best course of action, and they arrested him on May 5. More violence erupted, this time in the village of Dharasana, where police brutally attacked a group of nonviolent protesters. Civil disobedience continued until early 1931, when Mohandas was finally released from prison. Afterward, he met with the viceroy and for the first time was treated on equal terms.

The negotiations with Viceroy Lord Irwin did not produce any concrete steps toward self-rule for India or gain any major concession from the British. Nevertheless, Mohandas recognized the importance of this moment. He saw it as a turning point, both for himself and his country. *Time*, the American weekly news magazine, declared Mohandas to be 1930's "Man of the Year." In India, Mohandas became something of a folk hero. After the Salt March, he understood the power that the Indian people held in their hands. He praised his fellow countrymen for "acting courageously" and refusing to "submit so easily to unjust oppression." The Salt March also succeeded in drawing the world's attention to the plight of India. Afterward, the power that the British held over the people of India was never quite the same. Mohandas was now more determined than ever to wage his battle of "right against might" until India gained the freedom it so richly deserved.

# CHAPTER 4

# Father of the Nation

## Prelude to War

After his release from prison in 1931, Mohandas once again turned his heart and mind to Hinduism and how best to remove the practice of untouchability from its religious customs. He was convinced that political reform before social reform would only replace unjust British rule with unjust Indian rule. Many orthodox Hindus were outraged by his criticisms. Some saw his attacks on Hinduism as an attack on the nation. They burned *effigies* (images) of Mohandas and chanted, "Death to Gandhi!" Members of the INC who were not faithful Hindus questioned Mohandas's excessive concern with this religious issue to the detriment of the political movement of which he was undoubtedly the leader. "I stand thoroughly discredited as a religious maniac and predominantly a social worker," he answered them. He added, "One must do one's duty to the best of one's ability."

In September 1934, Mohandas resigned his membership in the Indian National Congress. Now 64 years old, he felt ready to step aside and hand the reins of power over to a younger generation of leaders. "It is not with a light heart that I leave this great organization," he said. Following this decision, he remained politically inactive for a couple of years. He then plunged into the struggle to help the millions of Indians who suffered from starvation and unemployment. He launched his All India Village Industries Association later that year. Two years later, Mohandas was convinced to return to politics when Jawaharlal Nehru reclaimed the presidency of the INC. Mohandas was reluctant to re-enter the political arena, but he did so to help resolve the conflicts among various factions of the Congress. He continued to refer to Nehru as his "heir" to national leadership, but the two men more and more disagreed about how to tackle the many problems facing India.

Around this time, Great Britain began to focus its attention on what was happening in Europe. In 1933, Adolf Hitler, leader of the National Socialist German Workers' (Nazi) Party, became chancellor of Germany. His rise to power was fueled by intense *anti-Semitism* (prejudice against Jews) and a call to do away with the Treaty of Versailles, which the Allies had imposed on Germany after its and its allies' defeat in World

*Some saw his attacks on Hinduism as an attack on the nation.*

War I. When asked what he thought of the persecution of the Jews in Germany, Mohandas replied, "My sympathies are all with the Jews. ...The tyrants of old never went so mad as Hitler." Before long, the possibility of war between the great powers of Germany and Great Britain seemed inevitable, and the world stood on the brink of another devastating conflict.

In July 1939, Mohandas wrote a letter to Hitler. Addressing him as "Dear Friend," as he did with political allies and opponents alike, Mohandas hoped to prevent the catastrophe of another world war. "You are today the one person in the world who can prevent a war which may reduce humanity to the savage state," he said. "Will you listen to the appeal of one who has deliberately shunned the method of war not without considerable success?" Unfortunately,

In 1939, Mohandas (above, wearing a shawl) arrived in Delhi to meet with Lord Linlithgow, the viceroy of India, after Britain declared war on Germany during World War II. Mohandas told the viceroy he could not support either side in the war.

Mohandas's plea was ignored. On September 3, Great Britain declared war on Germany in response to Germany's invasion of Poland two days earlier. Lord Linlithgow, who had become viceroy of India in 1936, immediately proclaimed India to be at war with Germany as well. In a meeting on September 4, Mohandas told the viceroy that his sympathies were with Great Britain "from the purely humanitarian standpoint." Though Germany was "responsible for the war," Mohandas said he could not, in good conscience, support either side. Not every Indian agreed with him, however. More than two million joined the British army and fought on various fronts during the six years of war.

The outbreak of World War II (1939-1945) served to unite the various factions of the INC in opposition to British rule. Nehru took the lead in drafting a resolution calling for Great Britain to include among its "war aims" granting full independence to India. Once this was agreed to, India's people would willingly cooperate in the struggle against fascism. (*Fascism* is an extreme form of authoritarian government that allows only a few people to run a country. Fascism involves total government control of political, economic, cultural, religious, and social activities.) Mohandas argued for a completely nonviolent response but won little support among the Congress's militant majority. Britain, of course, did not respond favorably to the Congress's proposition. Winston Churchill, who became prime minister of Great Britain in May 1940, never had any intention of negotiating an agreement with India while his country was at war. However, the viceroy, Lord Linlithgow, spent the next several years trying to win the support both of Mohandas and the Congress. At the urging of the Congress, Mohandas launched another campaign of Satyagraha against Britain's denial of India's dream of freedom and democracy.

In contrast to the Congress's response, Muhammad Ali Jinnah, speaking for the Muslim League, immediately assured the viceroy that Indian Muslims would loyally support the British war effort. Late in 1940, Mohandas learned that Jinnah was calling for a *partition* (division) of India once it gained its freedom from the British Empire. The new nation of Pakistan, the "Land of the Pure," would be a Muslim-majority country and pursue a completely independent course from the Hindu-dominated India. At first, Mohandas refused to take Jinnah's demand for a partition of India seriously. He thought Jinnah was using the idea of "Pakistan" as a bargaining chip to gain political leverage in an independent India. Mohandas would soon find out how serious Jinnah was. In the meantime, the tension between India's Hindus and Muslims grew deeper, taking a great toll of lives in both communities.

In June 1941, the scope of the war widened when Germany invaded what was then the Soviet Union. Six months later, Japan launched its surprise attack on the United States naval base at Pearl Harbor in Hawaii. The attack brought the United States into the war. When reporters asked Mohandas about the spread of the war across the globe and what it meant for India, he repeated his pledge to nonviolence. He said that if he were "viceroy of India today," he would not ask his countrymen to "take up the sword" to keep the British Empire alive. "I for one should feel that I was committing moral suicide … abandoning the faith of a lifetime," As the war progressed, his calls for the end of British rule in India only intensified. When the press asked Mohandas what he would do if the British refused to leave India after the war, he replied, "I shall have to force them to go, by noncooperation or by civil disobedience. Or it may be both." In the summer of 1942, Mohandas made plans for another campaign of Satyagraha. Its aim, as he put it, was "to secure the withdrawal of British rule and the attainment of independence for the whole of India." This was to be the last great Satyagraha of his career.

## The Quit India Movement

On August 3, 1942, Mohandas traveled to Bombay to meet with the All India Congress Committee, the decision-making body of the INC, and draw up a resolution demanding India's complete independence from Britain. Mohandas carried with him a confidential draft of instructions for those taking part in his Satyagraha campaign. He told the committee that every participant "should understand before joining the struggle that he is to ceaselessly carry on the struggle till independence is achieved" and that everyone should take a "vow that he will be free or die." Mohandas also coined a slogan for the campaign: "Do or die!" However, his last Satyagraha campaign soon came to be known as the "Quit India" movement. Before long, Indians were shouting this two-word phrase to every British soldier and civilian whose path they crossed. "The cry of 'Quit India,'" Mohandas wrote, "comes not from the lips but from the aching hearts of millions."

*"The emphasis in any nonviolent struggle … is always on peace."*

When Mohandas was asked by reporters if the INC's resolution meant "peace or war," he replied, "The emphasis in any nonviolent struggle … is always on peace." On August 7, Mohandas addressed the All India Congress Committee and told them that the British "will have to give us freedom when we have made sufficient sacrifices and proved our strength." When one of the committee members predicted that this Satyagraha campaign would take no more than a week, Mohandas said such a feat would be nothing less than a "miracle." To gain the widest base of support possible, Mohandas also called upon Muhammad Ali Jinnah and the Muslim League to join his campaign of Satyagraha. The following day, Mohandas reinforced his message of nonviolence by telling a British newspaper that he had "equal love for all mankind without exception." Speaking to the INC, he called for "freedom immediately, this very night, before dawn." That evening, the Congress unanimously passed his resolution. The British authorities were quick to respond, arresting Mohandas, his wife Kasturbai, and more than 50 leaders of the INC within hours. As he was taken away to prison, Mohandas raised his harsh voice so that everyone could hear him: "*Satyagrahis* [those taking part in a Sa-

Mohandas was deeply affected by the death in 1942 of his personal secretary Mahadev Desai (below, whispering in Mohandas's ear. Jawaharlal Nehru sits on the floor in front).

tyagraha] must go out to die not to live. … It is only when individuals go out to die that the nation will survive."

After Mohandas and the leadership of the INC were imprisoned, large demonstrations protesting their imprisonment took place across India. Some of the protests turned violent. Some 250 railways stations were attacked, telegraph wires were cut in the district of Bihar, and more than 100 police stations were burned to the ground, causing the deaths of around 30 officers. By the end of 1942, tens of thousands of Indians would be put in jail. More than 600 of them were subjected to public floggings. The official death count rose to 900. Many Indian leaders who were not arrested by the British went underground.

> *"It is only when individuals go out to die that the nation will survive."*

As India plunged into chaos, Mohandas remained a prisoner in the Aga Khan Palace in Poona for nearly two years. Though the palace was hardly a jail, in many ways it proved to be his most painful imprisonment. Mahadev Desai, who had served faithfully as Mohandas's personal secretary for the last 25 years, died of a heart attack on August 15 while being held at the palace. Desai was only in his early 50's, and his death deeply affected Mohandas. Only the day before Desai's death, Mohandas had written the viceroy, urging the British government to reconsider its actions. "Do not disregard the pleading of one who claims to be a sincere friend of the British people," he said. Lord Linlithgow, however, was unmoved by this heartfelt plea. By this time, Linlithgow shared Winston Churchill's view of Mohandas's "treacherous" nature.

Throughout this troubling period, Mohandas maintained his determination to oppose British tyranny through nonviolent means. He went on a 21-day fast in the spring of 1943, despite his failing health. After the fast ended on May 4, Mohandas felt a renewed sense of mission. He began writing to many British officials, including Lord Linlithgow, hoping to win back their trust. Once again, he reaffirmed his faith in nonviolence and expressed his hopes for peace, both in India and the world. However, nothing that Mohandas wrote produced a positive response.

*He simply did not understand how betrayed the British officials felt by his failure to support the Allies . . .*

He simply did not understand how betrayed the British officials felt by his failure to support the Allies (China, the Soviet Union, Great Britain, and the United States) in their war against the Axis powers (Germany, Italy, and Japan).

Around this time, Kasturbai's health began to fail while she was still a prisoner in the Aga Khan Palace in Poona. In January 1944, she suffered two heart attacks. After that, she spent most of her time in bed and in great pain. Drifting "between life and death" for several days toward the end, she passed away on February 22, 1944. Mohandas was at his beloved "Ba's" side when she died—they had been married for 63 years. Kasturbai was cremated in the same corner of the palace grounds as Mahadev Desai had been. At the funeral, Mohandas spoke briefly before his son Devdas lit the funeral *pyre*. (A pyre is a large pile of materials for *cremating* (burning) a dead body.)

On May 6, 1944, Mohandas was released from prison in the Aga Khan Palace on humanitarian grounds. His health was failing, and he required surgery. But Mohandas continued to call for the release of the INC leaders who remained in prison. By the time he returned to his ashram, a measure of peace had returned to India. Nevertheless, many nationalists expressed their disappointment in the Quit India movement. They felt that it had been a failure, and they criticized Mohandas and the INC for not accomplishing more. Mohandas took their criticism in stride. He was surprised to see how much the political landscape had changed during his imprisonment. The Muslim League, whose influence in India had been marginal only a few years before, now stood at the center of the political stage. Muhammad Ali Jinnah's campaign for an independent Pakistan was gaining momentum.

## Independence and Separation

In July 1944, Mohandas wrote a letter to Jinnah, referring to him as *Bhai* (brother). "Let us meet when you wish to," he said. "Please do not regard me as an enemy of Islam and the Muslims [in India]. I have always been a friend and servant of yours and of the whole world. Do not dismiss me." Jinnah replied the following month, inviting Mohandas to his home in Bombay that September for "frank and friendly talks" on the future of India. Despite their different beliefs, the two men had a profound respect for each other. Jinnah urged Mohandas to accept the idea of an independent Pakistan before the war ended. "We should come to an agreement and then go to the [British]," Jinnah said, "and … force them to accept our solution." Mohandas patiently explained how he saw the situation. "I agree the League is the most powerful Muslim organization," he replied, "but that does not mean all Muslims want Pakistan." By the end of the meeting, the two agreed that India and Pakistan should not "separate" until they reached a final agreement.

When Jawaharlal Nehru (who was still in prison) learned that Mohandas and Jinnah had met, he was "very much put out." He did not think that the division of India into two separate nations should be accepted quite so easily. In the end, Mohandas and the

Mohandas (right) and Mohammad Ali Jinnah of the Muslin League met for talks in Bombay (now Mumbai) in 1944 on the future of British-ruled India. Jinnah later became the first leader of the new nation of Pakistan.

INC proposed that the question of partitioning India be resolved with a direct vote in all districts with Muslim-majority populations. Not everyone was happy with this compromise. Nehru called it a "devil dance." Later in September, Mohandas and Jinnah met again. At this second meeting, their talks broke down. Jinnah held fast to the idea that two nations existed within British India—a Muslim state and a non-Muslim state. Both, he argued, had a right to self-determination. Mohandas, however, did not believe India should be divided along religious lines. He said, "I am unable to accept the proposition that the Muslims of India are a nation, distinct from the rest of the inhabitants of India." He added that the implications of Jinnah's ideas were "dangerous in the extreme." If such a proposition were accepted, he believed, "there would be no limit to claims for cutting up India."

Sir Archibald Wavell, who had become the new viceroy of India in late 1943, worked with the INC and the Muslim League to find common ground. Wavell was afraid that India would erupt into civil war, and he felt that neither Mohandas nor Jinnah would be able to stop it. During negotiations, his dislike for Mohandas was obvious. Mohandas's statements on the British Empire did not help matters. When World War II ended in 1945, Mohandas said that men like Winston Churchill were no less "war criminals than Hitler and [the Italian dictator Benito] Mussolini." In private, Wavell referred to Mohandas as a "malignant, malevolent, exceedingly shrewd politician."

Mohandas (fourth from right) takes one of his daily walks in 1946. He is joined by his two secretaries and some of his family members, including his son Manilal (left center).

In July 1945, elections were held in Great Britain. Winston Churchill's Conservative Party was voted out of office, and the more progressive Labour Party under Clement Attlee came to power. With the Labour Party victory, India's aspirations for independence suddenly seemed within reach. The following year, the British government under Attlee began the process of handing over the administration of British India to the Indian people. That December, Prime Minister Attlee invited both Nehru, who had by now been released from prison, and Jinnah to London for talks. Religious riots between India's Hindus and Muslims were becoming commonplace, and Attlee hoped to end the violence. Unfortunately, his efforts failed to bring Nehru and Jinnah any closer together. After the brief summit in London, Nehru flew home to convene India's Constituent Assembly in New

Delhi's new Parliamentary House on December 9. All seats belonging to members of the Muslim League remained empty, however, as Jinnah had organized a boycott.

In March 1947, the new viceroy, Lord Mountbatten, invited Mohandas to meet with him in New Delhi. Mohandas was depressed by the violence that continued to plague India and reluctantly agreed to a meeting. Mountbatten asked him if he knew any way to restore peace. Mohandas's response was for the British to ask Jinnah to form a national government as prime minister "and present his Pakistan plan for acceptance" before India's independence was proclaimed. This, Mohandas thought, was the "best solution" to all of India's problems. The suggestion took Mountbatten by surprise. When the viceroy shared the conversation with Nehru, he was told that Mohandas had been away from New Delhi for too long and that he was "out of touch." By the end of April, Mohandas understood that neither Mountbatten nor Nehru had any intention of following his plan to avoid the partition of India. Nehru was unwilling to let Jinnah have the power that came with being prime minister. Mountbatten, who liked and trusted Nehru, followed his counsel. "Whatever the Congress decides will be done," Mohandas commented. "No one listens to me any more. I am a small man."

*"No one listens to me any more. I am a small man."*

On July 17, 1947, Britain's Parliament passed the Indian Independence Act, authorizing the partition of India into two separate nations. The exact boundaries between India and Pakistan were to be drawn up by a commission of both Hindus and Muslims. The commission was led by Sir Cyril Radcliffe, a London-based lawyer who had never set foot in India. The partition was highly controversial and more violence followed. A mass migration also took place. Eventually more than 10 million people—Hindus, Muslims, and Sikhs alike—crossed the newly created borders to settle in the country of their choice. India's independence was officially proclaimed on August 15. The Indian people's long struggle to gain their freedom was finally over.

Mohandas spent August 15 in Calcutta. However, he did not spend the day celebrating India's independence or the end of British rule. Instead, he urged everyone to join him in a fast. A week later, Nehru asked Mohandas to bring his "healing presence" to the Punjab, a region of India that suffered terrible violence in the wake of independence and partition. Mohandas received dozens of other similar requests as the death toll in India and Pakistan continued to rise. Mohandas was deeply saddened by the loss of life. "We have drunk the poison of

Lord Mountbatten, the last viceroy of India (center), disclosed Britain's partition plans for India during a conference in New Delhi with Muslim League leader Muhammad Ali Jinnah (right) and Indian nationalist leader Jawaharlal Nehru (left).

mutual hatred," he complained. He urged his countrymen to be courageous in the face of their suffering, and he condemned "the idea of taking revenge on the Muslims." In response, many fanatical Hindus began calling him "Muhammad Gandhi" and made threats against his life. Mohandas was depressed and frustrated by the violence that gripped the subcontinent. But he never gave up hope that the madness could be ended. Unfortunately, his words of peace and harmony were ignored by far too many.

In 1947, when India was partitioned into two separate nations, a mass migration took place. Over 10 million people crossed the newly created borders to settle in the country of their choice: Hindu-dominated India or Muslim-dominated Pakistan.

## Assassination

In September 1947, Mohandas moved to Delhi to help stem the violence there. In October, he celebrated his 78th birthday. He observed the occasion by fasting. Later in the month, the violence that gripped India and Pakistan erupted into full-scale war. The war broke out when Pakistan sent its militia over the border to secure Kashmir, a region whose official status as being part of India or Pakistan or becoming independent had yet to be determined. Mohandas immediately urged Nehru to negotiate a settlement with Pakistan. "We should at least try to arrive at an agreement," he said. "Mistakes were made on both sides. ... But this does not mean that we should persist in those mistakes."

On January 20, 1948, a frail Mohandas spoke to supporters in the garden of his residence known as Birla House. "I have no doubt that one who is an enemy of the Muslims is also an enemy of India," he said in a weak voice. A moment later, a hand grenade exploded behind him, scattering the crowd. No one was hurt and the would-be assassin was arrested. Birla House was put under military guard. "I believe that Rama is my only protector," Mohandas declared. (*Rama* is a popular Hindu god. He usually is shown as a king carrying a bow and arrow.) Ten days later, Mohandas rose before dawn and performed his prayers, as usual. That afternoon, visitors began to arrive. Nehru was expected at Gandhi's residence sometime after evening prayers, which were scheduled for 5 p.m. About a quarter after the hour, with the assistance of his grandnieces, Manu and Abha, Mohandas headed toward the garden. He was running late that day.

As Mohandas made his way down the garden path, most of the people who had gathered there to see him bowed their heads and moved aside. However, one young man blocked his way forward. His name was Nathuram Godse. As Godse bowed before Mohandas, apparently wishing to touch his feet in a gesture of respect, one of his grandnieces said, "Brother, *Bapu* is already late." Godse then straightened himself, leveled a small automatic pistol at Mohandas, and fired three shots into his chest at point-blank range. Manu heard Mohandas mutter the words, "*Hei Rama*" (meaning "Oh, Rama" or "Oh, God"). As large bloodstains appeared on his white shawl, Mohandas fell to the ground. The Mahatma was dead.

Nathuram Godse made no attempt to escape. Mohandas's assassin was seized by nearby witnesses and quickly arrested. In the weeks that followed, several accomplices were detained as well. Godse was a Hindu nationalist who had ties to the extremist political party known as Hindu Mahasabha. At his trial three months later, Godse was defiant as he stood before India's High Court. "My provocation was his constant and consistent pandering to the Muslims," he said. "I declare here before man and God that in putting an end to Gandhi's life I have removed one who was a curse to India." Godse was found guilty and sentenced to death. Despite pleas of clem-

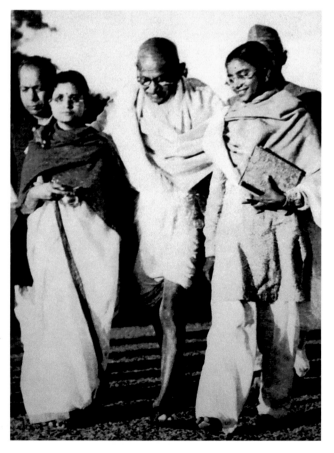

Mohandas is shown here with his grandnieces at his last public gathering on his way to evening prayers on Jan. 30, 1948. He was shot and killed as he headed toward the prayer meeting.

ency from Mohandas's sons Manilal and Ramdas, Godse was executed on November 15, 1949.

Prime Minister Nehru, addressing the nation on the radio, announced the news of Mohandas's assassination. "Friends and comrades, the light has gone out of our lives, and there is darkness everywhere, and I do not quite know what to tell you or how to say it. Our beloved leader, *Bapu* as we called him, the father of the nation, is no more." Mohandas's death was mourned across India. It served to unite India's government as well as untold numbers of Hindus, Muslims, and Sikhs. Millions of mourners gathered outside Birla House and the roads leading up to it, crying, "Long live Mahatma Gandhi!"

In 1948, Indians gathered in a room in India House in London for prayers for Mohandas during his fast for peace between Hindus and Muslims. Here, some paused before his portrait at prayer time.

The following morning, the five-mile-long funeral procession began. Mohandas's flower-covered body was placed on a gun carriage, which was led by four armored cars and followed by the governor-general's horse guard of lancers and 200 of India's finest soldiers. Mohandas's son Ramdas was given the honor of lighting the funeral pyre. It burned through the night, reducing the Mahatma's body to ashes. On February 12, those ashes were taken to the junction of the Rivers Ganges and Yamuna. There, according to Hindu tradition, the waters are said to wash away all of one's sins and free the deceased from the cycle of rebirth.

## Legacy

Today, India hails Mohandas Gandhi as the "Father of the Nation" and celebrates his birthday as a national holiday. His smiling face graces the country's currency. The leaders of India continue to lay wreathes on the ground where his body was cremated. Birla House, the place of his assassination, has become a museum, housing his last meager possessions and the bloodstained clothing he was wearing when he was murdered. The people whom Gandhi fought for, the poor and untouchables, gather outside the building every day to mourn him. Gandhi is perhaps best remembered for his decades-long struggle to liberate India from British rule and exploitation. But his legacy goes well beyond that great achievement.

Gandhi's message of peace and his devotion to the truth have inspired countless people throughout the world, including many important political, social, and religious leaders. Among them have been such luminaries as Martin Luther King, Jr., in the United States and Nelson Mandela in South Africa. King, who helped liberate American society from the injustice of racial discrimination, found Gandhi's life and work "profoundly significant" for himself and the civil rights movement in the United States. Before he too was struck down by an assassin's bullet in 1968, King came to see nonviolence as "one of the most potent weapons available to an oppressed people in their struggle for freedom." Mandela, South Africa's first black president, spent years in the same prison in which Gandhi had been held by the British. Mandela paid tribute to the Mahatma's impact on the world as well as his own life. "Though separated in time," he wrote, "there remains a bond between us, in our shared prison experiences, our defiance of unjust laws." He added that Gandhi's "nonviolent resistance inspired anticolonial and antiracist movements internationally."

Shortly after Gandhi's death, Albert Einstein, the great scientist, said of him: "Gandhi's life achievement stands unique in political history. … The moral influence he had on the consciously thinking human beings of the entire civilized world will probably be much more lasting than it seems in our time with its overestimation of brutal violent forces. … We may all be happy and grateful that destiny gifted us with such an enlightened contemporary, a role model for the generations to come. Generations to come will scarce believe that such a one as this walked the earth in flesh and blood."

# INDEX

# FURTHER READING

Gandhi, Rajmohan. *Gandhi: The Man, His People, and the Empire.* Univ. of Calif. Pr., 2008.

Lelyveld, Joseph. *Great Soul: Mahatma Gandhi and His Struggle with India.* Vintage Bks., 2012.

Lucas, Eileen. *Mahatma Gandhi: Fighting for Indian Independence.* Enslow, 2018.

Sawyer, Kem Knapp. *Mohandas Gandhi.* Morgan Reynolds, 2012.

# ACKNOWLEDGMENTS

Cover: © Elliott & Fry/Getty Images

3 © Universal History Archive/UIG/Getty Images

7-10 Public Domain

13 © Rühe/ullstein bild/Getty Images

16-22 Public Domain

25 © Dinodia Photos/Alamy Images

27 © Paul Fearn, Alamy Images

28-35 Public Domain

38 © Archive PL/Alamy Images

41 Public Domain

44 © Dinodia Photos/Alamy Images

47 © World History Archive/Alamy Images

49 Public Domain

51 © Dinodia Photos/Alamy Images

55 © World History Archive/Alamy Images

61 © Universal History Archive/UIG/Getty Images

62 © Keystone-France/Getty Images

66 National Library of France

69 © PA Images/Getty Images

71 © Margaret Bourke-White, The LIFE Picture Collection/Getty Images

74 © Hulton-Deutsch Collection/Getty Images

78 © Bettmann/Getty Images

82 © Universal History Archive/UIG/Getty Images

84 © Margaret Bourke-White, The LIFE Picture Collection/Getty Images

86 © Keystone/Getty Images

87 © AP Photo

89 © Universal History Archive/UIG/Getty Images

90 © AP/REX/Shutterstock Premier